The Wild Outdoors

GO HIKING!

by
Heather Bode

Captivate is published by Capstone Press, an imprint of Capstone.
1710 Roe Crest Drive, North Mankato, Minnesota 56003
www.capstonepub.com

Library of Congress Cataloging-in-Publication Data
Names: Bode, Heather L., author.
Title: Go hiking! / by Heather Bode.
Description: North Mankato, Minnesota : Captivate is published by Capstone Press, [2022] | Series: Wild Outdoor | Includes webography. | Includes bibliographical references and index. | Audience: Ages 8-11 years | Audience: Grades 4-6 | Summary: "What could be more fun than taking a walk through nature's wonders? Readers will learn all about the proper clothing, footwear, and supplies they need to go hiking in the wild outdoors. They'll learn about well-known trails and discover how to safely explore the natural world around them"— Provided by publisher.
Identifiers: LCCN 2021026318 (print) | LCCN 2021026319 (ebook) | ISBN 9781663906113 (Hardcover) | ISBN 9781663920539 (Paperback) | ISBN 9781663906083 (PDF) | ISBN 9781663906106 (Kindle Edition)
Subjects: LCSH: Hiking—Juvenile literature. | Hiking for children—Juvenile literature. | Day hiking—Juvenile literature. | Walking—Juvenile literature. | Outdoor recreation—Juvenile literature.
Classification: LCC GV199.52 .B64 2022 (print) | LCC GV199.52 (ebook) | DDC 796.51—dc23
LC record available at https://lccn.loc.gov/2021026318
LC ebook record available at https://lccn.loc.gov/2021026319

Summary: Introduces readers to the activity of hiking, including historical information on hiking and ways to do it safely.

Image Credits
Alamy: Chuck Little, 13, Lee Rentz, 26; Getty Images: duncan1890, 5; Shutterstock: BalanceFormCreative, 7, encierro, 14, Golden Pixels LLC, 8, Ho Su A Bi, 15, Joshua Resnick, Cover, m_sovinskii, 23, melissamn, 12, 19, MiniStocker, 21, Monkey Business Images, 11, 18, 29, rbkomar, 17, Rene Stevens, 1, roibu, 27, Sergey Tinyakov, 25, Steven Dominic, 9, Wandel Guides, 24

Editorial Credits
Editor: Mandy Robbins; Designer: Jennifer Bergstrom; Media Researcher: Jo Miller; Production Specialist: Tori Abraham

Printed in the United States 4694

Table of Contents

Words in **bold** are in the glossary.

Introduction

THE ADVENTURE BEGINS

Shhh. Did you hear that? The whisper of the breeze. A bird's song amidst rustling leaves. Listen. Nature calls to you, "Come and explore. I promise you adventure."

Hundreds of years ago, most people lived and worked in nature all the time. **Rural** societies focused on farming. But in the mid-1800s, something happened. An industrial age arrived with an increase in technology. People moved to cities and found factory and office work with long hours cooped up inside. Suddenly, they missed nature calling to them. Hiking became a popular escape.

Today, hiking is rising in popularity. It currently ranks as one of the top five outdoor sports. Are you ready for real-life adventure and exploration? Then it is time to take a hike!

An engraving shows two people hiking in the 1800s.

FACT

A recent study found that people who grow up participating in outdoor activities are more likely to keep doing those same healthy activities as adults.

Chapter 1

THE PERKS OF HIKING

Hiking is a sport many people enjoy. For most, no special equipment is needed. Going on a hike exercises your heart, lungs, and muscles. Working these organs increases **endurance**. As your endurance increases, you will be able to hike longer distances. Your **coordination**, balance, and flexibility will improve.

Being out in nature also exercises your mind. The quiet surroundings let you see plants and animals in their natural **habitat**. You may even find a new interest. Hiking often leads to hobbies such as bird-watching, bug and plant identification, photography, and more.

You never know what natural wonders you may spot on a hike.

Many adults enjoy hiking alone, but kids should always have a responsible adult with them. You can walk down a paved path, through an uncharted forest, or down a known dirt path. Bring friends or family members along too. You can enjoy the challenges of hiking together and point out different natural wonders to each other.

Sometimes hikers use a walking stick for extra support.

In some places, special signs mark hiking trails.

Hiking has other benefits too. You will gain self-confidence and build problem-solving skills as you decide which hiking paths to take. You can choose more and more difficult paths as you become an experienced hiker. Every time you complete a hike, you achieve your goal.

Chapter 2

HIKING HOW-TOS

Hiking trails are found almost anywhere. Some are paved and twist through local parks or wooded trails. Others are found in national forests, state parks, national parks, and nature preserves. Trails may follow beaches, forests, canyons, and mountains. The **geography** where you live determines the types of trails you use.

If you know experienced hikers, ask them where to go. Or start at a local state or national park. Ranger stations and visitor centers there have helpful maps. You could also take a trip to the library to find a hiking guidebook of your area.

Hiking can be a fun family activity.

Hikers set off to explore Hidden Lake Trail at Glacier National Park in Montana.

Start with easy trails of 0.5 to 2 miles (0.8 to 3.2 kilometers) and work up to longer trails. You can even add hills. This helps build your endurance. If you're a morning person, take a hike as the sun rises. At that time of day you are also well rested and will have the most hours of daylight.

Guidebooks show you different types of hikes. A destination hike takes you to a location such as a waterfall, a lake, or an overlook. A loop hike makes a full circle where you see new **scenery** all along the way. An out-and-back hike means you retrace your steps on your way back to where the trail begins. This point is called a trailhead.

A guidebook can help you plan your hike.

Hiking can be done in every season. Summer is the busiest time for hiking because it has the warmest weather. But spring and fall are also great times for hiking. There are usually fewer people out then. In some places, changing tree blossoms and leaves are beautiful these times of year.

Hiking when it's warm may require bug spray and sunscreen.

In cool climates, winter hikes in snowshoes give you the chance to make footprints in freshly fallen snow. Even though you might not see much wildlife, you will know they are there from the tracks they leave.

Some people use special poles to help them hike through snow.

When Not to Hike

Even when everything is carefully planned, you might need to delay a hike. If severe weather is coming your way, it is safer to stay home. Getting trapped in a storm, tornado, or heat wave is very dangerous. Sometimes trails are closed due to animals, mud slides, or fallen trees. Swarming mosquitoes may make you change your mind. Stay positive, knowing there will be another day for your next hiking adventure.

Chapter 3

SAFETY AND SUPPLIES

Hiking requires few supplies. Shoes or boots are the most important equipment. Make sure they have good grip on the bottom and are comfortable to wear. Apply sunscreen before you head out and bring more if you're planning a long hike.

Long hikes also require a backpack, so you can bring plenty of water and any other supplies. Since weather can change quickly, add an extra sweatshirt or jacket to the backpack. A small first-aid kit is handy for scraped knees and cuts.

Don't forget the snacks! Food gives you energy to keep hiking. Some common hiking snacks are cheese sticks, crackers, granola bars, dried fruit, candy, and nuts.

Make sure you bring plenty of water for your hike.

FACT

Did you know feet are one of the sweatiest parts of your body? Together they can produce up to 1 cup (240 milliliters) of sweat each day! To prevent sticky, stinky feet, bring an extra pair of socks to change into on long hikes.

Staying on the trail keeps you safe from tripping hazards and dangerous plants, such as poison ivy or poison oak.

Hiking is a fun way to get exercise, but it is still important to stay safe. Keep your eyes on the trail. There may be uneven surfaces and tree stumps, rocks, and other tripping hazards. Sometimes branches hang lower than you expect, so watch your head.

Make sure you stick with your group or a trusted adult. Hike in small groups so you don't hog the trail. Always keep each other within eyesight. Choose the right **pace**, or how fast you will move along the trail. Wear bright-colored clothing, which makes you easy to spot. Bring a map so you know the trail. Many maps are available online, so you can see them on a smartphone.

If you're hiking where there is cell service, you can use a smartphone to map your route.

Trail Games

Hiking can be quiet and peaceful. It could also be a fun time for games! Try some games to keep the hike interesting.

- ☑ I Spy: One hiker calls out, "I spy with my little eye, something __________." Choose one word to describe your object. Then see if others can spy it too!
- ☑ Follow the Leader: While keeping safety in mind, the lead hiker changes body movements as he or she hikes. Other hikers follow the movements of the leader.
- ☑ Scavenger Hunt: Before the hike begins, make a list of items to find for the hunt. Ideas include a pine cone, bugs, wildflowers, or squirrels.
- ☑ Shape Shifter: Find something in nature that looks like something else. Maybe it's a branch in the shape of a letter! Once you spot a shape shifter, point it out to fellow hikers.

Chapter 4

THE INVISIBILITY GAME

Now that millions of people are making use of trail systems, we must be **global citizens**. Global citizens understand how to take care of the outdoors. You may have heard phrases such as, “Leave No Trace,” or “Pack It In, Pack It Out.” These sayings help us remember our responsibility to nature. Think of this as the invisibility game. Did you leave evidence that you were on a trail? If you answer, “No,” then you win!

Certain tips can help you win the invisibility game. Hike on **durable** surfaces. Always stay on marked trails. Avoid taking shortcuts because this causes **erosion**. Erosion gradually destroys a surface. Fertile soil can be washed away.

A sign reminds hikers to respect the trails.

FACT

In the United States, national parks are popular destinations for hikers. There are 59 national parks in the country. In 2019, an estimated 1.46 million people visited them every day!

Healthy snacks can keep your energy up for a long hike.

Anything you bring into nature must leave with you. Food, bandage wrappers, and tissues must not be left on trails. Garbage attracts animals, and this endangers the well-being of both animals and hikers.

On the flip side, remember to leave what you find. Sometimes hikes take you past old buildings, flowering meadows, or slopes filled with sparkling rocks. It is tempting to take something you find on a hike. But if every hiker takes something out of nature, what will be left? If you're going to take anything, take a photo. This allows you to remember what you see without removing it. Think of the next hikers, who will be amazed by the same objects you have already enjoyed.

Photos let you remember your hike without disturbing the environment.

Remember to keep in mind that you're not the only creatures out on the trail. Be aware of animals. As amazing as it is to see animals in their natural habitat, always remember to watch them from a safe distance. Stay back and leave no food. It's healthier for wild animals to find their own food.

Be alert of certain times of the year when animals may be more sensitive. This includes when they have babies in the spring and summer or as they are preparing for winter. Again, instead of trying to get too close to an animal, take a photo instead—or even a video!

Animals on well-traveled trails may not be afraid of humans.

A marker called a blaze guides hikers.

FACT

Many trails have markers called blazes. They can be painted markings on trees, flags, signposts, or even piles of rock. See how many blazes you can find as you blaze your own trail!

Chapter 5

HIKE BY THE RULES

Safety rules aren't the only rules hikers need to follow. There are also certain types of manners called hiking **etiquette**. These manners make it easier to share the trails.

Hiking Etiquette

- ☑ Hike in small groups rather than large ones.
- ☑ Like cars on roads, stay to the correct side of the trail. In some countries this is the right side, and in others it's the left.
- ☑ It is OK to talk while hiking, but speak quietly so other hikers can enjoy the sounds of nature.
- ☑ If someone catches up to you, let them pass.
- ☑ If you catch up to someone, let them know you are there. Greet them and ask if you may pass.
- ☑ Downhill hikers **yield** to uphill hikers. If you are hiking down an incline and you meet other people coming up, step aside to let the uphill hikers pass before you continue down.

Now that you know the basics, get out there and take a hike! No matter where or when you do it, hiking gives you adventures and experiences you will remember long into the future.

GLOSSARY

coordination (koh-OR-duh-nay-shun)—the ability to control body movements

durable (DOOR-uh-buhl)—able to last a long time

endurance (en-DUR-enss)—the ability to keep doing an activity for long periods of time

erosion (i-ROH-zhuhn)—the wearing away of land by water or wind

etiquette (ET-ih-ket)—rules that outline proper behavior

geography (jee-OG- ruh-fee)—the study of Earth's surface and its land and water features

global citizen (GLOH-buhl SI-tuh-zuhn)—any person who takes responsibility for taking care of nature

habitat (HA-buh-tat)—the natural place and conditions in which a plant or animal lives

pace (PAYSS)—the speed at which you move

rural (RUR-uhl)—having to do with the countryside

scenery (SEE-nur-ee)—the natural countryside of an area, such as trees, hills, mountains, and lakes

yield (YEELD)—to stop and allow someone else to go

READ MORE

Andrews, Kim. *Exploring Nature Activity Book for Kids: 50 Creative Projects to Spark Curiosity in the Outdoors.* Emeryville, CA: Rockridge Press, 2019.

Morey, Allen. *Hiking.* Mankato, MN: Amicus, 2017.

Siber, Kate. *National Parks of the USA.* Minneapolis: Quarto, 2018.

INTERNET SITES

American Hiking Society
americanhiking.org/

Leave No Trace: Welcome to PEAK Online!
lnt.org/get-involved/training-courses/peak-online-course/

Top 10 Family-Friendly Hikes in the U.S. Parks
nationalgeographic.com/adventure/lists/hiking-backpacking/family-friendly-hikes/

INDEX

WWW.APEXEDITIONS.COM

Apex is distributed by North Star Editions:
sales@northstareditions.com | 888-417-0195

Produced for Apex by Red Line Editorial.

Photographs ©: Erik Kabik Photography/MediaPunch/IPX, cover, 1; Shutterstock Images, 4–5, 6, 7, 8–9, 14, 15, 16–17, 18–19, 20–21, 22–23, 24, 25, 27, 29; Thomas Nelson/British Library/Flickr, 10–11; American National Red Cross/Library of Congress, 12–13; iStockphoto, 26

Library of Congress Control Number: 2021915743

ISBN
978-1-63738-157-1 (hardcover)
978-1-63738-193-9 (paperback)
978-1-63738-263-9 (ebook pdf)
978-1-63738-229-5 (hosted ebook)

Printed in the United States of America
Mankato, MN
012022

NOTE TO PARENTS AND EDUCATORS

Apex books are designed to build literacy skills in striving readers. Exciting, high-interest content attracts and holds readers' attention. The text is carefully leveled to allow students to achieve success quickly. Additional features, such as bolded glossary words for difficult terms, help build comprehension.

SURFING

APEX

By Mary Boone

TO LEARN MORE

BOOKS

Doeden, Matt. *Could You Be a Monster Wave Surfer?* North Mankato, MN: Capstone Press, 2020.

MacDonald, Lisa Steele. *The Science of Waves and Surfboards.* Huntington Beach, CA: Teacher Created Materials, 2019.

Scheff, Matt. *Surfing.* Minneapolis: Abdo Publishing, 2021.

ONLINE RESOURCES

Visit **www.apexeditions.com** to find links and resources related to this title.

ABOUT THE AUTHOR

Mary Boone has skydived, ridden an elephant, and baked cricket cookies—all in the name of research for magazine articles and books. She lives in Tacoma, Washington, and has written more than 60 nonfiction books for young readers.

INDEX

Answer Key:
1. Answers will vary; **2.** Answers will vary; **3.** A; **4.** B; **5.** A; **6.** C